5/09

Staying Safe

Safety at School

By MaryLee Knowlton
Photography by Gregg Andersen

Crabtree Publishing Company

www.crabtreebooks.com

Crabtree Publishing Company

www.crabtreebooks.com

Author: MaryLee Knowlton
Project coordinator: Robert Walker
Editor: Reagan Miller
Proofreaders: Molly Aloian, Crystal Sikkens
Production coordinator: Katherine Kantor
Prepress technicians: Samara Parent, Ken Wright, Margaret Amy Salter
Design: Westgraphix/Tammy West

Written, developed, and produced by
Water Buffalo Books/Mark Sachner Publishing Services

Photographs: © Gregg Andersen/Gallery 19

Acknowledgments:
The publisher, producer, and photographer gratefully acknowledge the following people for their participation in the making of this book:
In Soldotna, Alaska: Dallas Armstrong, Mary Armstrong, Chris Kempf, Er Kempf, Jackie Kempf, Etta Mae Near, Jerome Near, Janet O'Toole, Mike O'Toole, John Pothast.
In Mankato, Minnesota: Debbie Benke, Candee Deichman, Liz Goertzen, Syndie Johnson, Brianna Ostoff. And a special thanks is offered to the dozens of school children, staff, and parents who gave generously and enthusiastically of their time and talent in the making of this book.

Library and Archives Canada Cataloguing in Publication

Knowlton, MaryLee, 1946-
      Safety at school / MaryLee Knowlton ; photography by
Gregg Andersen.

(Staying safe)
Includes index.
ISBN 978-0-7787-4317-0 (bound).--ISBN 978-0-7787-4322-4 (pbk.)

      1. Schools--Safety measures--Juvenile literature. 2. Safety
education--Juvenile literature. I. Andersen, Gregg II. Title.
III. Series: Staying safe (St. Catharines, Ont.)

LB2864.5.K56 2008   j613.6   C2008-905552-7

Library of Congress Cataloging-in-Publication Data

Knowlton, MaryLee, 1946-
   Safety at school : by Marylee knowlton ; photography by Gregg Andersen.
      p. cm. -- (Staying safe)
   Includes index.
   ISBN-13: 978-0-7787-4322-4 (pbk. : alk. paper)
   ISBN-10: 0-7787-4322-5 (pbk. : alk. paper)
   ISBN-13: 978-0-7787-4317-0 (reinforced library binding : alk. paper)
   ISBN-10: 0-7787-4317-9 (reinforced library binding : alk. paper)
   1. Schools--Safety measures--Juvenile literature. I. Andersen, Gregg. II. Title. III. Series.

   LB2864.5.K58 2009
   363.11'9371--dc22

                                                              2008035387

Crabtree Publishing Company

www.crabtreebooks.com   1-800-387-7650

Published in Canada
Crabtree Publishing
616 Welland Ave.
St. Catharines, ON
L2M 5V6

Published in the United States
Crabtree Publishing
PMB16A
350 Fifth Ave., Suite 3308
New York, NY 10118

Published in the United Kingdom
Crabtree Publishing
White Cross Mills
High Town, Lancaster
LA1 4XS

Published in Australia
Crabtree Publishing
386 Mt. Alexander Rd.
Ascot Vale (Melbourne)
VIC 3032

Contents

Words in **bold** are defined in the glossary on page 30.

Staying Safe at School

Every day, you have to make choices about your own safety. Whether you are at home, at school, at a playground, or around water, staying safe is something you must always think about.

In this book, each section presents a school safety **hazard** or problem.

Here is how the book works:

First, you will read about a school safety problem.

Second, you will choose how to solve the problem.

Third, you will learn about the **consequence**, or outcome, of each choice.

For every bad consequence, you will see a "no" sign.

For every good consequence, you will see a gold star.

Finally, you will learn which is the best choice and why.

You will learn ways to stay safe at school and on the bus. Telling your friends what you learn will help them make safe choices, too.

Throwing Things in the Classroom

It is important to share with our classmates. If a classmate needs a pencil or piece of paper, it is helpful to share. What if a classmate who needs something is sitting a few seats away from you?

What is the quickest and safest way to pass something to your classmate?

What's happening?

Your friend Devonta calls from two tables over, "Hey, Scott. Can I borrow your dictionary?"

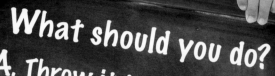

What should you do?

A. Throw it to another friend and let her toss it to Devonta.

B. Toss it over the heads of the kids sitting between you. She can catch it!

C. Walk over to Devonta and hand her the dictionary.

Which is the best choice?

Turn the page and find out!

What happens next:

If you choose A . . .

Your throw is off. The book hits Madison and lands in her work. 🚫

If you choose B . . .

Devonta isn't paying attention. The book could hit her and hurt her. 🚫

No mess. No fuss. No one gets hurt!

The best choice is C.
Walk over to Devonta, hand her the book, and keep your classroom safe!

What have you learned?

Throwing things in class can hurt other people and spoil their work.

Running in the Hall

Being careful in the hall helps keep everyone safe. You know you shouldn't push and shove.

But how safe can you be if you are in a hurry? How safe are the people around you?

What's happening?

The bell has rung and your friends are waiting for you on the playground. You don't want to miss a minute of fun! What's the best way to get out of school fast?

What should you do?

A. Run through the hall with your arms out so people will move.

B. Run through the hall yelling for people to get out of your way.

C. Walk toward the door without pushing and yelling.

Which is the best choice?

Turn the page and find out!

What happens next:

If you choose A . . .

While waving your arms, you could hit another student in the face. 🚫

If you choose B . . .

The other kids in the hall may not be able to move out of your way and you could trip over them or their books. 🚫

If you choose C . . .

You get where you are going
without hurting yourself or anyone else.

The best choice is C.

Walk carefully in the halls and you will get
where you need to go safely without missing
any of the fun!

What have you learned?

Running indoors can hurt other children
and you, too. Walking is the safest and
quickest way to get where you need to go!

No Joking about Choking!

Lunch can be a great time to talk to your friends about what you did last night or to make a plan for after school.

How can you talk and still finish eating before lunchtime is over?

What's happening?

You can't wait until lunch is over to tell your friend Mitzi about the video game you got for your birthday. But you've got a mouthful of food.

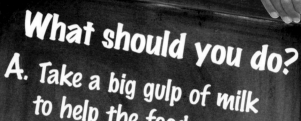

What should you do?

A. Take a big gulp of milk to help the food go down faster.

B. Chew and talk at the same time.

C. Chew carefully and swallow your food and tell Mitzi your news before you put anything else in your mouth.

Which is the best choice?

Turn the page and find out!

What happens next:

If you choose A...

The milk makes you cough and choke. Your friends are grossed out when you spit your food out and milk comes out of your nose! ⊘

If you choose B...

The food could get stuck in your **windpipe** as you try to talk and eat at the same time. You could choke! ⊘

Your food ends up where it should be—in your stomach, and not on the table or stuck in your windpipe. Your friends can look at your smile instead of your chewed-up lunch!

The best choice is C.

Chew carefully and swallow your food before you talk or put anything else in your mouth.

What have you learned?

Talking with food in your mouth and trying to eat and drink at the same time is dangerous and gross. Take the time to chew and swallow carefully.

Beware of Stairs!

Accidents on the stairs can really hurt. Getting from one floor to another at school can be tricky with all the kids and the teachers trying to get somewhere else at the same time!

That's when you have to act safely for yourself and also for others.

What's happening?

You have to get to your classroom, but the kids from your little sister's class are ahead of you on the stairs. Those little kids are so slow!

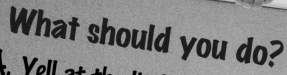

What should you do?

A. Yell at the little kids to hurry up and give them a little push to nudge them along.

B. Pass them and run down the stairs.

C. Hold onto the railing and walk down the stairs.

Which is the best choice?

Turn the page and find out! ....▶

What happens next:

If you choose A . . .

Your yelling and pushing might scare the children and cause some of them to stumble and fall. 🚫

If you choose B . . .

You crash into someone coming up the stairs and you both get hurt. 🚫

20

You and the little kids make it down the stairs.

The best choice is C.
Hold onto the railing and walk down the stairs.
Safety, not speed, matters most
when using the stairs.

What have you learned?

Hang onto the railing, walk carefully, and don't
ever push on the stairs. Set a good **example**
for other children, especially younger ones.

Bringing Dangerous Things to School

Showing things from home to friends at school can be fun if your parents and the teacher know about it first.

Do you know the rules about what kinds of things can be brought to school?

What's happening?

Your friend David's dad has a Swiss army knife with a lot of really cool **attachments** on it. David has brought it to school to show you.

What should you do?

A. Tell David to show the knife to other kids. They will think it is cool, too.

B. Tell David that he should keep the knife hidden from other people, so he doesn't get in trouble.

C. Tell David you will go with him to tell a teacher about the knife.

Which is the best choice?

Turn the page·········· and find out!

What happens next:

If you choose A . . .

One of your friends could cut himself with the knife. ⊘

If you choose B . . .

David might accidentally cut himself with the knife. ⊘

Nobody gets hurt. David learns the consequences of breaking the rules, but he also learns how to keep himself and others safe.

The best choice is C.

If David doesn't want to go with you, then you should tell the teacher yourself. The teacher will make sure David understands the importance of keeping everyone safe in school.

What have you learned?

Keeping safe is more important than keeping out of trouble. Knives are not toys and should never be brought to school.

Don't Cause a Fuss on the Bus!

Sometimes kids act badly on the school bus. This can be dangerous for everybody. The driver can try to keep order on the bus, but his or her first job is to drive safely.

How can you help keep the bus safe?

What's happening?

Two boys are punching and kicking each other on the bus.

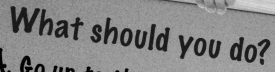

What should you do?

A. Go up to the driver and tell him about it.

B. Go over to them and try to pull them apart.

C. Do not get out of your seat. Let the driver know there is trouble by calling to him from your seat.

Which is the best choice?

Turn the page and find out!

What happens next:

If you choose A . . .

While you are out of your seat, the bus might come to a stop, and you could fall and hurt yourself and others. 🚫

If you choose B . . .

You might get hurt while trying to break up the fight. You could end up getting punched! 🚫

The bus driver stops the fight while everyone else remains safe in their seats.

The best choice is C.

Stay in your seat and stay safe on the bus. It's the driver's job to break up fights, not yours!

What have you learned?

Don't become a flying object when the bus stops or turns quickly! You will be safe if you stay seated. Also, when people fight you may not be able to fix things right away. But you can always talk to your teacher about anything that makes you feel unsafe.

Glossary

attachment A part or piece that is connected to something

consequence The result or effect of an action; something that happens as a result of something else happening

example An object or a kind of behavior that shows others what something is like or how something is done

hazard A danger or a chance to get hurt

nudge To push someone gently

windpipe The tube in our bodies that goes from the back of the mouth through the throat and into the lungs. Air enters and leaves our lungs through the windpipe

BOOKS

At School (Safety First). Helena Attlee. Franklin Watts, 2004.

Safety on the School Bus. Lucia Raatma and Karen E. Finkel. Bridgestone Books, 1999.

Staying Safe at School (Safety First). Joanne Mattern. Weekly Reader Early Learning Library, 2007.

Staying Safe on the School Bus (Safety First). Joanne Mattern. Weekly Reader Early Learning Library, 2007.

WEBSITES

Safe-a-Rooni
http://www.safe-a-rooni.org/
A fun site with games, guides, and activities about safe play. Do them online or download and print them out.

School Safety with McGruff
http://www.mcgruff.org/Advice/school_safety.php
Great advice and activities for staying safe at school and traveling to and from school.

Kids.gov: The Official Kids' Portal for the U.S. Government
http://www.kids.gov/k_5/k_5_health_safety.shtml
This site provides information and activities that teach and encourage safety. It also includes an amazing list of links to other sites about safety.

Index

Printed in the U.S.A.